YOUR FIRST SERMON

YOUR FIRST SERMON

Getting from Here to Sunday in Five Manageable Steps

GARY NEAL HANSEN

Climacus Publishing

Copyright © 2020 by Gary Neal Hansen

All rights reserved.

No part of this book may be reproduced in any form or by any electronic or mechanical means, including information storage and retrieval systems, without written permission from the author, except for the use of brief quotations in a book review.

Scripture quotations marked (NIV) are taken from the Holy Bible, New International Version®, NIV®. Copyright © 1973, 1978, 1984, 2011 by Biblica, Inc.™ Used by permission of Zondervan. All rights reserved worldwide. www.zondervan.com The "NIV" and "New International Version" are trademarks registered in the United States Patent and Trademark Office by Biblica, Inc.™

New Revised Standard Version Bible, copyright 1989, Division of Christian Education of the National Council of the Churches of Christ in the United States of America. Used by permission. All rights reserved.

Paperback ISBN: 978-0-9864124-6-2

Ebook ISBN: 978-0-9864124-7-9

For the Rev. John Duff

And how can they hear without someone preaching to them?

> — ST. PAUL, ROMANS 10:14 NIV

I can do all this through him who gives me strength.

> — ST. PAUL, PHILIPPIANS 4:13 NIV

CONTENTS

Introduction	xiii
1. STEP ONE: GETTING YOURSELF READY	1
Getting Your Head Ready	1
Getting Your Heart Ready	6
2. STEP TWO: CHOOSING YOUR TEXT	9
Talk to Your Pastor	11
Option One: Lectionary Preaching	11
Option Two: Series Preaching	12
Option Three: Topical Preaching	13
3. STEP THREE: STUDYING YOUR TEXT	17
1. Break It Down	19
2. Look It Up	24
3. Focus on Details	29
4. Distill the Essence	31
4. STEP FOUR: LISTENING FOR REAL-LIFE CONNECTIONS	35
Avoiding Common Pitfalls	36
Exercise 1. Dive in a Bit Deeper	37
Exercise 2. Take Your Text for a Walk	41

Exercise 3. Write Some Stuff Down	43
Exercise 4. Listen for the Message in Your Culture	46
5. STEP FIVE: BRINGING IT ALL TOGETHER	49
The Goal: Four Specific Pages	50
Page One: Tell the Story	52
Page Two: Explore the Problems	55
Page Three: Show Connections to Life and Culture	60
Page Four: Emphasize God's Call to Us	65
6. STEP SIX: ACTUALLY PREACHING IT	69
1. Print It Legibly	70
2. Use the Pulpit	71
3. Practice	72
4. Try Out That Pulpit in Advance	74
5. Speak to the Last Row	75
6. Give Yourself Permission to Be Nervous	76
7. Find a Friendly Nodder	77
8. Then Stop	78

Afterword	81
Suggestions for Further Reading	83
Acknowledgments	85
Other Books by Gary Neal Hansen	87

INTRODUCTION

Here's my guess: Your pastor asked you to preach the sermon next week, and you are sweating bullets. I mean, hey, of course you are flattered. It's great that a pastor you respect has enough confidence in you to ask you to cover on a vacation week. But on the other hand, yikes! You don't like public speaking much. You've never even thought about how to prepare a sermon.

Well, I have two words for you. To quote that esteemed theological resource *The Hitchhiker's Guide to the Galaxy*, "Don't Panic." Better still, two words from the Apostle Paul: "Rejoice always!"

Here's why you should rejoice: It is fantastic that you will be preaching. It is something worth doing—a crucial part of your congregation's worship life, and quite possibly a very important moment for one or many of the people who will listen to you.

Here's why you shouldn't panic: God is on your side—and it is God who has the most investment in preaching. You see God's priority on preaching right there in the New Testament, from John the Baptist and Jesus preaching about the kingdom of Heaven to Paul telling us that preaching is the standard way people will hear the gospel and come to salvation. Even if you are nervous about doing the work of preaching this week, know that God is working behind the scenes to help you succeed.

Also, I'm here to help. My job is to get you all the way to Sunday morning in five manageable steps. (Then there's a sixth bonus step to get you through actually preaching your sermon.) You can totally do this.

Notice that I called the steps "manageable." I did not say they would be drop-dead easy. You will need to do the work. But preparing and preaching a sermon is not rocket science. It can be broken down into steps that you can understand and follow, leading to a solid and worthwhile result.

But let's be clear: I'm not aiming to turn you into a rock star of the pulpit overnight. My goal is to help you prepare and preach a sermon that is faithful to Scripture, helpful to the congregation, and an accomplishment you can be proud of.

WHY THIS BOOK?

There are lots of books on preaching out there by famous preachers, so why should you read this one?

First, those other books are not written for you. Some are textbooks for seminary classes. Some are guides for experienced pastors to improve their preaching. Some are scholarly studies that would only interest professors of preaching. This book, on the other hand, is written with *you* in mind: a nervous first-time preacher.

Second, those other books are too long. You only have until Sunday. You can't spend the whole week reading a preaching book. You need time to prepare that sermon. By contrast, this book is blessedly short. If you were to just read it, instead of actually doing the steps I tell you about, you would probably be done in about half an hour.

Third, you need practical step-by-step guidance. That's often the best approach to learning a new and complex skill. This book will give you the very basic steps you need. When you learn to cook, you start with a basic recipe. Later, you can improvise and build on the basics. If you want to think of preaching as an art, you can become Michelangelo later. For now, just paint by the numbers.

But why, you ask, should you listen to me?

First, I'm an experienced preacher. I'm an ordained minister in the Presbyterian Church, and we Presbyterians take preaching really seriously. I served as a pastor for years, preaching hundreds of sermons.

Second, I'm an experienced teacher. For nearly two decades I was a professor at a theological seminary. Along the way I won my university's highest teaching award. I've taught a lot of people who became ordained pastors and lay pastors.

Third, I have a PhD in church history. Now don't yawn. The relevant thing about that is that I can take the long view about what has made the best preaching effective over the last two thousand years.

Fourth, I may just be the only game in town. As of the time I'm writing, this little book of mine is the only one written for people in exactly your situation. Whether you end up liking my approach or not, it will give you a place to start.

IF YOU WANT MORE HELP

Before we dive in, let me note one important thing, and make you an offer.

Different people learn differently. If you

find that working through this book on your own is too impersonal for your learning style, I invite you to check out the online preaching course I offer at my website. It has the same title as this book, and you'll find it at this address: "https://bit.ly/PreachingClass". The course is short and quite affordable, and it follows the same approach as the one in this book. However, in the course I teach through video lectures and step-by-step homework. Plus, if you want even more help, I offer options that include getting feedback on your sermon manuscript before you preach it, or even a personal coaching call to help you prepare it.

At the end of this book you'll find coupon codes to purchase the video course at a significant discount. You'll probably find the discount is more than the price of this book, so you will be no worse off for having started here. In fact, people often find that having both a book to read and videos to watch helps them deepen their learning.

So, are you ready?

Let's do this!

STEP ONE: GETTING YOURSELF READY

The first step toward being ready to preach next Sunday won't sound like "working on your sermon." Getting ready to preach starts before you write a single word. Being ready to prepare your sermon, *really ready*, doesn't take a lot of time, but it does require some very specific work in your head and your heart.

GETTING YOUR HEAD READY

First the head. Let's focus on the goal of a sermon. If you don't know where the journey is supposed to end, you are very unlikely to get there, whether you are going for a drive or planning a sermon.

So, what is a sermon?

If you were to study a whole bunch of sermons by the most influential preachers in history, you would find that they consistently did two things.

1. They explained the biblical text that was read in the service.

2. They helped people see how that biblical text related to real life—the lives of real Christians in their community and their culture.

On the other hand, over the years when I've listened to sermons that didn't succeed, usually they seemed to stumble on one of those same two issues.

Issue 1: Failure to Explain the Text

Some of the preachers left the biblical text completely in the dust and talked about something else.

Other preachers brought in so many different biblical texts to illustrate their points that I couldn't remember what the main text even was.

Issue 2: Failure to Relate It to Real Life

Some preachers presented a thorough Bible study of the chosen text, but never touched on why it matters for Christian living.

Other preachers tried to apply the biblical message, but they related it to problems that seemed totally made up—not like my actual struggles, or like those of anyone I know.

Aiming for the Target

Here's some good news: Your sermon isn't going to have any of those problems. Why? Because right from the beginning you are going to point your sermon toward the right destination. You know how maps usually have a grid drawn over them so you can find a particular place by coordinates on the X and Y axes? Well, you are going to choose the right map coordinates as the goal of your sermon:

X Axis: You are going to say something helpful about the biblical text.

Y Axis: You are going to relate that biblical text to life as we know it.

Switching to an archery metaphor, you are going to aim at the right target. That means you will at least come close to hitting the target on your very first try. And if you are at least close to the target, your listeners are going to be very forgiving. No kidding.

Having a Biblical Text

Stop and think about the first of those two coordinates. I have assumed you actually have a text, and somebody is going to read it to the congregation. If you are in a church with centuries-deep roots, this is a no-brainer. Traditional Christian worship always includes reading one or more passages from the Bible.

On the other hand, you may come from

a church that does not have this custom. Still, no problem. Even if your congregation does not expect it, you, as the preacher, can choose to start off by reading a passage of the Bible to them. Please do this. You'll make your own life as a preacher so much easier, and we both want this to be as easy and successful as possible.

Notice: Your text is a passage *from the Bible*. That means your sermon is not your own life story. When you stand up in front of the congregation and tell the story of how you came to Christ, that is not actually a "sermon." That's called "giving your testimony." Giving your testimony is a great thing, whether to a friend or to a congregation, but that is not what is traditionally meant by a sermon. If your pastor asked you to give your testimony next Sunday, that's great, but I'm afraid this book won't help you much. (Sorry! The final bonus step will still be helpful.)

Using your testimony as your first sermon is also a potential longer-term problem. If you get asked to preach a second time, you have already used up your material. The Bible is a far richer resource for preaching material. Plus, unlike your life and mine, the Bible is the word of God.

A sermon is not actually about you. It is about God's message in Scripture, and it is about your congregation's life of faith. That makes the task more weighty. You'll need to get to know that text and listen for what God is saying and doing in it. And you'll need to communicate about the passage, helping people understand it and how it relates to their lives.

And that, my friend, is really important stuff. It's like the scene between Frodo the Hobbit and Aragorn the Ranger in the movie version of Tolkien's *The Fellowship of the Ring*. Poor little Frodo has a quest to undertake, and Aragorn asks him, "Are you frightened?" "Yes," says the Hobbit. The Ranger looks at him seriously: "Not nearly frightened enough." This Sunday you won't be sent to pitch a magical ring into the flames of Mount Doom, but you do have an important quest. Someone's spiritual life and salvation may hang in the balance.

It isn't just that the Bible is the word of God, more powerful than any magical ring. As Heinrich Bullinger, one of the most important theologians of the Protestant Reformation, put it, *preaching* the biblical message actually *is* the word of God. Imagine that: What you say next Sunday could be God's own word. That might make your knees knock, if you weren't anxious enough already. Or, if you aren't careful, it might give you an unhealthy ego boost.

The thing to remember is that preaching is not the word of God because you are so smart or so important that God made you his mouthpiece. No. Preaching a sermon on Sunday morning is God's word precisely because the people come to worship God, to speak to God in prayer, and to listen to what God is saying to their lives. *You* are working hard to explain a passage of Scripture to the people in a way that connects to living the Christian life. *They*, on the other hand, are *listening to God* by listening to the Bible and how its message matters. In fact, they are listening more closely and more prayerfully than you probably want to know.

GETTING YOUR HEART READY

And you? Your job is to listen to God as well. This is why, as well as getting clear concepts about preaching into your noggin, you need to get your heart ready for preaching. Another, even more influential theologian of the Reformation, John Calvin, would tell you that to get anything useful out of your reading and study of the Bible, you need the help of the Holy Spirit. To Calvin, the Bible is like a pair of glasses that enable us to see God and God's ways clearly. But without the Holy Spirit, we are like people sitting in a dark room. As you've probably noticed, even the best glasses don't help in the dark. We need to pray for the Spirit to shine God's clear light into our darkness. That's actually why, in worship services in the Reformed tradition, before they read the Bible or preach from it, they say a "prayer for illumination" asking the Holy Spirit to shine some light in our hearts and minds so we can see, hear, and understand what God is trying to get across in the Bible.

And that's the key first step to getting your heart ready for the actual work of preparing your sermon. You need to pray, asking God's help, asking God's Holy Spirit to shine in your heart and mind, helping you see what God is doing and hear what God is saying. For one thing, it puts you in the appropriate stance: humility. When you are humble, you know the sermon is not about your life, or even about your own wisdom. You realize the whole process is about coming to the Bible to learn what God is saying so that *you* can grow in faithfulness. Then, after humbly listening and responding yourself, your sermon can be of service to God's people.

It's good to be humble. It's even okay to feel personally inadequate to preach God's word, though there is no need to run away in terror. Calvin was right: We really do need God's help to do this effectively. That's not a crisis though, because God is there to help. The best way to get that help is to ask. With God's help, you really can do this. And I'm here to help too. All the steps to come are quite manageable. Just remember that you are on holy ground.

Pray for God's help. That's your task for step one. Then turn the page.

STEP TWO: CHOOSING YOUR TEXT

The second step also probably won't take much time, but for some new preachers it's emotionally fraught: You have to decide on the topic of your sermon. I've already pointed out that the subject of a sermon is a biblical text. That means your subject can't be your own life or your own wisdom. You need a text. But maybe knowing that your sermon needs to be on a passage from the Bible doesn't narrow it down all that much. I mean, hey, the Bible is a really long book.

This was the quandary I wrote about in the blog post that became so popular that it prompted me to create an online preaching course, and later prompted me to write this book. I told the story of the seminary student who had been asked to preach his first sermon. He looked up a wise old pastor to help him figure out what to do.

Seminarian: "Pastor it's my first sermon. What should I preach about?"

Wise Old Pastor (thoughtfully): "Well, you should preach about . . . Jesus." (Pause.) "And you should preach about . . . fifteen minutes."

It's a joke, but those are actually pretty good guidelines. The coming chapters will help you figure out how to fill up about fifteen minutes. For now, we'll focus on the "preach about Jesus" part.

The wise old pastor was guiding the seminarian to choose a text from the Gospels—Matthew, Mark, Luke, and John, the books that tell stories about Jesus. That's really helpful advice. If you choose a passage from the Gospels, especially if it is a story, you are making your work as a preacher easier, and you are making it more likely that the sermon will help your congregation. Jesus is your role model in this: Think about how often his own teaching and preaching took the form of stories. Whether you preach a story about Jesus in action, or a story that Jesus told, it is easier to say something helpful about a story than to wrestle with a dense bit of Paul's teaching. It's likely to be helpful to the people because the whole of the Christian faith comes down to living in response to Jesus; a Gospel text will put your attention, and the congregation's attention, right where it needs to be.

- But which Gospel will you choose?
- Which chapter of that Gospel?
- Which passage from that chapter?

TALK TO YOUR PASTOR

Before you choose a text, I recommend you talk to your pastor. Whether you have a burning passion to preach on a particular text, or whether you haven't got the slightest clue, the experienced preacher who asked you to do this can help you. He or she may have good suggestions on what text to choose. You may even find that he or she already expects you to preach on some particular text.

Start by finding out how your pastor chooses a text each week. It will probably be one of three approaches.

OPTION ONE: LECTIONARY PREACHING

Most mainline Protestant churches use what is called "the Revised Common Lectionary." A lectionary is a fixed, official, or at least approved, schedule of biblical readings. Some denominations require preachers to use the lectionary. For others it's optional.

If your pastor recommends you use the

lectionary, it narrows your choice of texts to four possibilities. For each Sunday of the year, the lectionary provides an Old Testament reading, a Psalm, a reading from the Letters, and one from a Gospel. Without the lectionary, you could choose anything between Genesis and Revelation, so hopefully winnowing down the options feels helpful.

My advice is for you to use the Gospel text assigned by the lectionary. Choice made. Easy-peasy.

OPTION TWO: SERIES PREACHING

Many pastors prefer to preach a series of sermons on a topic. They pick passages each Sunday to fit the overall purpose of the series. That frees you up from the constraints of the lectionary, and allows you to plan based on the needs of the congregation.

Series preaching is a great way for a pastor to use the pulpit for a teaching ministry. In the past I've preached sermon series on the Lord's Prayer, the Ten Commandments, the Apostles' Creed, and other topics. A series can be on a biblical topic like parables or miracles, or on themes of the Christian life, like faith or relationships. In the Reformed Tradition (that's churches with "Reformed" or "Presbyterian" in their title), preaching through a book of Scripture from beginning to end is the classic way to create a sermon series.

If your pastor says he or she is in the middle of a series, that may come with a suggestion that you take up a particular passage so that your sermon fits into the flow. If so, your decision about what text to preach suddenly became very clear.

OPTION THREE: TOPICAL PREACHING

In some churches, things aren't so preplanned. Each sermon flows from the pastor's sense of what the Holy Spirit is prompting at that particular moment. Pastors still tend to preach from a biblical text, but they choose that text to emphasize a point that they believe God wants the congregation to hear. If that's what your pastor says, then you have a whole lot of freedom about Sunday's text.

That may feel like a bit too much freedom. You may find it paralyzing to have to pick your own text from anywhere in the Bible, or you may not feel confident that you can hear the Spirit's whisper. Here's my advice: Narrow your choices by one of the following approaches.

1. If there is a *joyful*, *gentle* Gospel passage that you know well and really love,

then use that. You'll be in comfortable territory.

On the other hand, if your favorite passage relates to a pet peeve, and your sermon would condemn that peeve, then please choose something else. "Gospel" means "*good* news." If you are at all tempted to present the bad news of judgment, you won't be preaching the gospel. And really, for your first time in the pulpit, preaching the good news of Jesus is your best path to success.

2. Find out what the lectionary Gospel is for your Sunday and just go with that. Choosing the lectionary text is perfectly fine even if your church doesn't normally follow it. In fact, nobody else needs to know the passage is from the lectionary. It's in the Bible, so it is fair game.

Would the Spirit really be likely to say "Anything *except* the lectionary passage please!"? I suspect the Spirit would be more likely to whisper, "Don't spin your wheels about which passage to preach. Make the easy choice and spend your time working on your sermon text. Hey, it's your first time!"

Preaching a text you did not personally choose can be a very good thing. You aren't just making your life easier. You are being humble. You won't be imposing your pet issues on the congregation, and you will show that you take all of Scripture seriously. You'll wrestle with the text and be pleasantly surprised how relevant and helpful it turns out to be.

3. If all else fails, go with one of these Gospel tests: The wedding at Cana (John 2:1–11), the calling of Zacchaeus (Luke 19:1–10), the woman caught in adultery (John 8:2–11), or Jesus blessing the children (Matthew 19:13–15, Mark 10:13–16, Luke 18:15–17). All are rich, full of grace, and bring more surprises than you might expect. You'll have fun working on any of them, and the congregation will be blessed with good news.

Okay, you have your assignment.

- Call your pastor for input and advice.
- Make your decision.
- And no matter which Gospel text you choose, it is going to be fine.

When you have your text, we'll move on to step three.

STEP THREE: STUDYING YOUR TEXT

At step three, you take your text and study it. In my experience, step three is the most fun, though I won't be shocked if you find it a bit intimidating. I know "study" sounds like "school," and maybe you didn't enjoy school that much. Lots of people don't feel they are good at studying. But if you avoid studying Scripture, you miss out on much of the joy that is to be found in the Bible.

One helpful trick is to rename the process. Use a less scary word. Try calling it "asking questions." That works well because that's what study actually is. Whatever the topic, if you are asking questions and looking for answers, you are studying. You start by asking little questions. You find answers to your little questions, then you ask more of them, until you discover answers to your big questions.

If you are asking questions about a passage of Scripture, and you keep asking questions, along the way you will discover a lot of amazing things. Some of what you discover will be puzzles and problems. That's good—these can lead you to still more questions to explore. Plus, your puzzles will be very useful in your sermon. Answering your questions and solving your puzzles will produce insights—into God, yourself, or the Christian life. These insights are good too. Not only are they really satisfying to come up with, but some of these insights will be the heart of your sermon. Together, your puzzles and your insights are what make your sermon helpful.

You don't have to be a Bible expert to ask questions. You may feel like your pastor can study a passage in more depth than you ever could. Well, seminary training and multiple years of preaching give your pastor a head start. However, that doesn't mean that you can't learn some wonderful, useful things about your passage starting right where you are. Just ask some questions and see where the answers take you.

That's the plan: Start where you are and take the steps you can. The key thing is to use the time you have to study the text in the most efficient and effective ways possible.

I recommend you spend a couple of

hours studying your text. If you were a full-time pastor, or if you had weeks and weeks before you had to preach, you would surely spend more time on this. Remember, though, I'm assuming you have to preach this coming Sunday. You have to do what is possible—so *some* study is better than *no* study.

You may be worrying about using your limited sermon preparation time this way. Shouldn't you be writing the sermon before you run out of time? Actually, no. All this study time is important preparation. You won't be actually writing your sermon yet. These two hours of study are crucial. They give you what you need to have on hand when you do start writing.

How are you going to spend these two hours?

I have four things for you to do.

1. BREAK IT DOWN

I don't preach every week these days, but every Monday I start studying a Gospel text as if I were preaching. I write a weekly article for my blog on the lectionary Gospel reading for the coming Sunday. It goes up under the heading "Monday Meditation," and on a typical week a couple hundred people, mostly pastors, read it. (That's another good reason to go with the lectionary Gospel. You can read my meditation as part of your study.)

How do I start? I break down the text.

I go to a web-based Bible site like Bible Gateway or Oremus Bible Browser. I look up my text in the translation I want to use. I copy and paste it into a blank word processor file. Starting with the text in its normal paragraph form, I use line breaks and tabs to divide it into thought units and clauses. It ends up with the ragged look of free-verse poetry. This is quirky, I admit. But it is also easy and super helpful.

This is probably easier to understand by seeing an example, so take a look at Figure 1.

18 As he walked by the Sea of Galilee,
  he saw two brothers,
    Simon,
      who is called Peter,
    and Andrew
      his brother,
        casting a net into the sea—
          for they were fishermen.
19 And he said to them,
  "Follow me,
    and I will make you fish for people."
20 Immediately
  they left their nets
    and followed him.
21 As he went from there,
  he saw two other brothers,
    James
      son of Zebedee
    and his brother John,
      in the boat with their father Zebedee,
        mending their nets,
          and he called them.
22 Immediately
  they left the boat
    and their father,
      and followed him.

Figure 1, Matthew 4:18–22 NRSV

Then I read through the passage very slowly. At the end of every phrase unit, I make a line break using the "return" key. If the next phrase is still in the same sentence, I hit the "tab" key so the second phrase comes below and to the right of the first. The next phrase goes one line down from that, tabbed in one step farther. Each sentence becomes a stair-step journey down the page and to the right. When a new sentence starts or a new speaker starts to talk, I go back to the left margin for a new set of stair-step phrases.

If a longer sentence has two or three related items in a row, those ideas all get indented the same number of tabs so they show up directly above and below each other. In passages of the psalms or the prophets this can capture the structure of Hebrew poetry, which makes its points through parallel phrases. But even in non-poetic passages, like most of the New Testament, this allows me to see the logic of repetitions and parallels.

When I look at the text this way I see it much more deeply. Conversations begin to jump out clearly, with their speeches showing as separate stair-step structures. Teachings of Jesus begin to reveal more of their meaning as his comparisons and contrasts show up on parallel lines.

To break down the text, you have to ask dozens of little questions.

- What is this phrase:

introduction, scene setting, or dialogue?
- Is this bit of dialogue related to the previous bit?
- Does this phrase continue the last thought, or does it start something new?
- Does this phrase modify the previous one?
- Is this thought parallel to that one?

Asking all those questions is like looking at the text under a microscope—and it is really easy. Also, it helps me see other questions I might want to think about in relation to the text.

Once I've broken the text down, I understand it much better than I did before. I see its hidden structures. It may be an odd process, but it illustrates what I said about study. It reveals puzzles and prompts insights.

That is, the process helps me see key words, repeated vocabulary, and odd turns of phrase that I might otherwise gloss right over. Those repetitions, emphases, and oddities are often really important to hearing Jesus' point in a text. Plus, you need to notice key words and words you don't quite understand so you can move on to step two of the study process.

But don't just read about my weird way of breaking down the text. Go do it. Break down your own text. Use your line breaks and tabs to ask questions and find interesting answers. Without working very hard, you will find you have actually studied the text in a really useful way. Even if the process seems foreign or uncomfortable, you'll see the text better, and you'll hear God's word more clearly. You will need that clarity to be ready to write your sermon.

Once you've broken the text down to make its structure visible, you'll be ready for the second step in your two hours of study.

2. LOOK IT UP

Hopefully in the process of breaking the text down you noticed a number of things. Maybe there were people mentioned, either individuals or groups. There may have been places mentioned—towns, regions, cities, or locations in Jerusalem, perhaps. There may have been some words that sounded like technical terms, like "justified," "crucified," or "sacrifice."

The next important-but-quick step in your time of study is to look up those terms. You, or your church's library, may have a

Bible dictionary or a Bible handbook. These will give you little articles on people, places, and things in the Bible. They are great resources, but if you don't happen to have them handy, Wikipedia is your friend. The quality of articles on Wikipedia varies, but since you only have a couple hours, make good use of what is in reach.

You also can learn very interesting things by looking up these interesting names and terms in a concordance. Like an index to every word in the Bible, a concordance will show you every passage where your word is used. Looking up a few of your passage's key words will often reveal interesting things. Perhaps a place mentioned in your text occurs in some important Old Testament story or prophecy. Other times, seeing how the same word was used by different writers in different contexts can shed light on nuances of its meaning. (No concordance? Use Bible Gateway or Oremus Bible Browser to provide the same information.)

My advice, then, is to spend some time with reference works. Look up the hard words. Look up unfamiliar people, places, and things. See where the words appear elsewhere in the Bible, just in case the Gospel is quoting or pointing to a particular Old Testament text. As C. S. Lewis put it in *An Experiment in Criticism*, "Find out what the author actually wrote and what the hard words meant and what the allusions were to, and you have done far more for me than a hundred new interpretations or assessments could ever do."

One strong suggestion: Do this bit of study on your own, rather than reading Bible commentaries. That is, you only have a couple hours. Invest it in digging for answers in the text itself, rather than skipping study and relying on other people's analysis. Discovering for yourself the meanings of the words within the larger context of Scripture is going to lead to a much richer understanding that will take you much further in your journey to Sunday's sermon.

If you are unfamiliar with the term, a commentary is a book written about a particular book of the Bible, usually by a Bible scholar. The author will take the book of Scripture and explain it, chapter by chapter, verse by verse, sometimes even word by word. There are many commentaries available for any book of the Bible, and the writers take many different approaches. Some are highly technical, analyzing Greek and Hebrew vocabulary and grammar, comparing differences in the various ancient Bible manuscripts, or looking for the influence of other literature from the biblical era. Preachers also write commentaries, sometimes developing them from their sermon series.

I have nothing against commentaries. There are lots of really good ones. People who preach regularly generally know which ones they find useful, and for what kinds of issues. As you prepare your very first sermon, though, I suspect commentaries would do you more harm than good.

Why? You might take your message from the writer of the commentary and fill your sermon with quotations instead of sharing your own raw insights. Your sermon will seem to be saying, "I don't know much, but this other guy does. Here's what he said."

Just saying what someone else said in a commentary leads to at least two problems. First, the congregation is going to be bored silly by commentary quotations. Second, relying on the commentary will erode your own confidence as a preacher. Your own study is what leads to clarity about the text. You could spend the whole week reading commentaries and never gain the confidence you would have from two hours of studying the passage yourself. Plus, if you are focusing on what the author of the commentary said, you might be distracted from what the Spirit is whispering about what your congregation needs to hear from your text.

If you read a commentary before you study, you might stop thinking and never go on to really engage with the text. It is too easy to assume that the really smart person who wrote the commentary has given you the one true meaning. That is way too much to ask of a single commentary, or even several.

On the other hand, let's say you do invest your energy into studying the text yourself. You get all excited about your discoveries, but then you think, "I'd better make sure I'm on the right track." You take a quick peek into a commentary just to buttress your confidence. Then, someone with all the authority of a Ph.D., says that the "real" meaning is something totally different from what you were about to preach. One minute you were happy and ready to roll. The next minute you feel as flat and soggy as a popped balloon.

Actually, in any given passage of Scripture there are layers of meaning; one could faithfully preach many possible messages from the same text. To preach well, you need to be personally invested in one particular meaning you dug up for yourself. With only one sermon to preach, and only one week to prepare it, you are better off without commentaries.

3. FOCUS ON DETAILS

The third step, once you've broken the text down to see its structure, and after you've looked up all the obvious key words, is to take a bit of time to focus on the details. Chances are, you have noticed some very interesting stuff in the passage. Now you need to give a little time and attention to looking closely at those interesting pieces. And then you need to dig for more. There is treasure in your text. All you need is time and some simple tools to find it.

First, print out your text as you broke it down in the first step of study. It should fit on a page or two with lots of white space all around it. (What? You didn't break your text down yet? Go do it. I'll be right here waiting.)

Second, get some writing tools—at least a pencil and a pen, plus colored pencils or highlighters if you have them. You need multiple tools so you can make different kinds of marks on different sorts of interesting details. If you have just a pencil and pen you can at least make two colors of circles and two colors of underlines.

Third, jot down some phrases that summarize the interesting things you've noticed so far. Put each little note near the part of the text it relates to. Keep doing this as new thoughts occur to you. The writing itself is helpful, even in these tiny bits. The more you write, turning your thoughts into words, phrases, and sentences, the better off you will be. Why? Writing something down forces you to think about it more clearly. It also helps you turn feelings or ideas into phrases and sentences you might want to use in your sermon. Every observation you write down is the answer to a question, whether you knew you were asking one or not. And when you have lots of answers written down, you can begin to see which ones seem most important.

Fourth, use your pens and pencils to ask some very intentional questions. With one, read through the text and mark all the names and pronouns so the people on stage begin to jump out. Take another color and mark all the verbs so you can see the actions. Is this text about walking, seeing, speaking, touching, or what? With another color, or another kind of mark, observe all the description words—adjectives, adverbs, or phrases that add color and feeling to the passage.

Is any of this leading to new observations? Write them down in the white space.

Now look for repetitions and other patterns. Connect them with lines. If you find more odd and surprising details, mark them too. Write down some more notes about anything that occurs to you during the process.

This process doesn't need to take a long time to be helpful. You might just find it is pretty fun and want to spend more time at it. That's great, as long as you have the time to spend. You may need to press forward, though, since this is your sermon week.

4. DISTILL THE ESSENCE

Now you are ready for the last step of our streamlined study process. You could, of course, spend a lot more time studying the passage. Chances are, someone out there has written a whole doctoral dissertation on it. But becoming an expert on the text is not the point. You need to study the passage only as long as it takes to be able to preach it confidently and faithfully. So just one more step. You need to distill what you have found down to its essence.

Even if you only have five minutes left on your allotted two hours of study time, this one is crucial. Frankly, if you've already gone over the two hours you planned to study, this one is so important you need to take an extra five minutes to do it.

Take a minute to read your text one more time. Then look through all the highlights, underlines, circles, and all the notes you wrote in the margins. Then ask yourself a question:

"What is *one thing* that this text is trying to get across about the life of faith?"

Notice that I did not say to ask "What is *the* one thing this text is trying to get across?" There is probably more than one. Don't even try to look for the *most important* thing the text is trying to get across. You just need to name *one thing* that you, in your own study, found useful, challenging, hopeful, helpful, or otherwise important.

By the way, not everyone would agree with me on this. A lot a people writing about Scripture would say you need to find *the one true meaning* of the text, that every text *has only one* meaning, and that you *can and must* find it and preach it.

I think those people are wrong.

Every time I write an article on a Gospel text (and like I said, I do it every week) I find at least three different potential messages, any of which would make a good sermon. Way back when, it was quite normal to look for multiple kinds of messages in any given text of Scripture. The same passage might tell us something about God in history, about our moral and ethical life, about theology or doctrine, and about heaven.

When the Spirit's light shines on a passage of the Bible, it is like when the sun shines through a prism. Suddenly plain ordinary light breaks apart into the separate bands of color you see in a rainbow. So, is the light really red? Is it also yellow? Is it also purple? Yes, and every color in between.

Of course a story about Jesus has many different points to make. He's God in the flesh. He's more complicated than we are. We shouldn't expect his actions or words to be simplistic. Every emphasis you find in a story about Jesus or by Jesus could become a different sermon.

So, take a couple minutes and distill your many observations down. Complete one of these sentences:

- One thing I *learn about Jesus* in this passage is . . .
- One thing I *hear Jesus calling me to do or be* in this passage is . . .
- One thing I *learn about the Christian life* in this passage is . . .
- One thing I *learn about the Church's life and mission* in this passage is . . .
- One thing I *find really challenging* in this passage is . . .

You don't need to complete all of the sentences. Just answer the one that helps you put into words the way the text has an impact on you personally. If your study leads you to a clear answer for any one of these questions, that is plenty. But write it down. You need to be clear with yourself about it. Writing it out will give you something crucial for the rest of your sermon-planning process.

Hey look, you've done it! You've studied Sunday's text, and you've come to a conclusion about what God is saying to you through it. That's going to be the core message of your sermon. Now, with that confident sense of the text and its message, you are ready for the next step.

STEP FOUR: LISTENING FOR REAL-LIFE CONNECTIONS

After doing all that good work studying the text and distilling it down to a really important message, you may think it's time to start actually writing your sermon.

Not so fast, grasshopper.

You'll do the actual writing when you get to step five, and it is going to be pretty easy because you are taking steps three and four so seriously. (You are taking these steps seriously, right?)

Your job in step four is to listen to the text with your life. You need to find connections between the message you just distilled and your own Christian life.

Don't jump yet to connections between the text and your congregation. Letting the text speak to your own life first will keep you humble. Telling other people how this message relates to them is a pretty bold step. You need to listen deeply and let God's message rattle around in your own soul first. And of course, finding connections to your own life will eventually help you think of how it relates to other people, to the church as a whole, or to society.

My goal in this whole process is to help you write a sermon that is genuinely helpful to the listeners. That is the best kind of success.

AVOIDING COMMON PITFALLS

Finding connections to your own life also helps you avoid some very common ways that sermons of new preachers fall flat. I've heard a lot of sermons by seminarians, and many that didn't succeed seemed to stop short at exactly this point. They showed that they had studied and found good things in the text, but then one of three things happened, any of which left the listeners scratching their heads.

1. Some stopped short of being a helpful sermon by just giving a Bible lecture. Good work on the text, but nothing at all to connect it to our lives. Ho hum.

2. Some turned everything into a command (which seemed to automatically include a bit of condemnation) telling us what we should do more of or less of. That sounds bossy pretty quickly. And it may mean the

preacher has found a non-Christian meaning in the Christian Scriptures. The Christian life is not always about obeying commands. More often it's about grace, and faith, and hope, and love.

3. Still others tried to connect the message to Christian living, but the Christian life they connected it to sounded completely unfamiliar. These preachers solved problems I didn't have or presented challenges I didn't face. In short, the sermons sounded completely unrealistic. The result? Listeners may end up figuring that passage of Scripture just doesn't apply to them personally. That's pretty sad.

Avoiding those pitfalls is easy if you do step four. I'm going to lead you through some pretty simple processes to help you make connections between the text and your own life so you can, appropriately and graciously, help the congregation connect with it too.

EXERCISE 1. DIVE IN A BIT DEEPER

The first thing I want you to do is to take a few minutes, no more than half an hour, to connect with the text in a way very different from what we did in step three. You've already studied the text with your thinking brain. Now you need to connect with it using the rest of you —your feelings and your imagination.

Back in the sixteenth century, a Roman Catholic spiritual guide named Ignatius of Loyola took spiritual seekers on retreats to try and find God's will for their lives. These weren't little weekends or overnights. Ignatius' retreats lasted a full month: four weeks to listen hard for the voice of God.

Day after day he led them through a process called the "prayer of the senses." First, he made them study a biblical story, as you have just done. Then came something new: Ignatius would have them meditate on the story over an extended period of time, using their imagination and their senses to enter it deeply and personally.

For the first hour they would go through the story imagining everything their eyes would have seen if they had actually been there.

Then in their second hour with the text, they would imagine what their ears would have heard if they were there.

A third hour of meditation would involve imagining what they would have smelled and tasted.

For the fourth hour they would imagine what they would feel in their bodies using their sense of touch.

By the end of those four hours they

would be so fully immersed in the story that they could approach Jesus in their prayerful imagination, or whoever else was in the scene, and talk about their problems and life questions.

That's a much bigger process than you have time for right now (though if you want to explore it, you will find a chapter on it on my book *Kneeling with Giants: Learning to Pray with History's Best Teachers*).

Here's a super-short adaptation—let's say ten minutes to half an hour. I want you to take a little time to go back through your text.

- Have a pen and paper ready.
- Imagine the story moment by moment, using all of your senses.
- Jot down phrases for what you imagine seeing, hearing, smelling, tasting, and feeling.
- When you are done, write at least a couple of complete sentences about your new observations and insights.

You have probably already done some of this. It's hard to spend time on a Gospel narrative and not let your imagination fill in some of the details that the text doesn't mention. Your task now is to do it on purpose, thinking clearly about everything that must or might have been happening in and around that scene. Writing some of that stuff down moves it from unconscious to conscious, and to something much more intentional and thorough.

The Bible lends itself to this. Compared to a novel, all biblical stories are lean on details. Your mind fills in the gaps, and when you tell the story, those details make it more vivid. You must have heard preachers do this, embellishing a Bible story with emotions or expressions that really aren't in the text.

That's natural, and maybe even necessary. If you had been there with Jesus when it all went down, there are countless things your eyes would have seen but that aren't mentioned. There were clothes, buildings and furniture, facial expressions, tones of voice and body language, maybe farm animals, whatever.

And there would have been countless sounds to be heard—murmuring crowds, rustling garments, shuffling footsteps, animal sounds, you name it.

And think of the smells—food, wine, bodies, fields, and dusty roads. Plus, those farm animals I keep mentioning.

The sensory details of every passage will be different. And your list of sensory details on any passage will be different from mine. That's okay. Neither one of us is claiming that we *know* what was there to be seen or heard. But we both get a much more vivid, engaged understanding of the passage by imagining it in full detail.

I want you do all this to spark a deep, gut-level connection to the text, emotionally and even physically. A good preacher isn't a disembodied brain. Only when you dive deep into the text with your senses and feelings can you invite other people to connect with it more deeply. You'll be telling the story, as well as talking about it, in your sermon. The richer your storytelling is with evocative details, the more you will help other people connect with the text. That's crucial to helping them see its relevance for their own Christian journey.

EXERCISE 2. TAKE YOUR TEXT FOR A WALK

Imagine your mind as a soup pot. To make soup, you need to put at least two ingredients in the pot and bring them to a simmer —you know, like meat and water. The meat is the story you studied. The water is your life story. Simmer them together and you'll get a good hearty broth. (I know, you need salt and vegetables too. Bear with me. It's just a metaphor.)

Here's one approach that may help. So far, you have studied the text. On top of this, you've done the imaginative exercise with your senses to expand your physical and emotional connection to the text. Now take a piece of paper and write down two questions.

First: "When did I *experience* something like that?"

Second: "When did I *feel* something like that?"

Next fold up the piece of paper, hold it in your hand, and go for a walk—around the block, out in the woods, whatever works. On the first half of your walk, think through your text from beginning to end, several times. You've spent enough time with it that you may be close to having it memorized. Tell the story in your head, over and over.

Every time you get to the end of the story, unfold the paper and take a look at it. Ask yourself those two questions. Then fold it back up, walk, and tell the story again.

Once you reach the halfway point of your walk, you can stop retelling the story. Walk and enjoy the world. Bring the story and the questions along. Don't try to think too hard.

Simmer, simmer, simmer. See what bubbles up.

EXERCISE 3. WRITE SOME STUFF DOWN

When you get back from your walk, find some paper or your journal. I want you to write a bit about the text and your life. Of course, not everybody likes to write, and some people run away screaming from the idea of keeping a journal. Take heart: You don't need to write something beautiful or profound. You don't even need to write everything in complete sentences. You just need to get some of what is in your head and your heart outside yourself and onto the paper.

I'll recommend an initial writing process for you, with some optional journaling tasks to follow.

Initial Writing Process: Three Little Tasks

I strongly recommend you do this first process. It is a way to summarize what you've done so far and prompt yourself to make life connections. There are three straightforward steps.

First, list your observations. Start by simply writing down thoughts, ideas, and feelings you found through your study and your sensory exploration of the text. List them out. Bullet points are fine, but try to get as long a list as you can—ten or twenty is better than two or three.

Second, summarize one takeaway. State clearly what you came to think of as one useful or interesting message from the text back at the end of the study step. This one should be a complete sentence.

If it helps, complete this sentence: "One thing this passage of Scripture teaches me is . . ."

Third, list life connections. Write a list of ways this message connects with your life.

- You could write about things that came up during your walk.
- You might think of times *in your past* where this message would have helped.
- You might come up with *current struggles* where this message brings a comfort or a challenge.
- Or you might think about *future scenarios* that you could shape with this message.

Write as many of these things as you can, and as specifically as you can. Nobody else needs to see what you've written. You might even throw it out afterward.

Optional Journaling Tasks

First, if you are comfortable journaling or want to give it a serious try, look back to the message you found in the "Initial

Writing Process" above. *Take that process as a prompt and just write about it*. Explore how taking that message seriously would impact your life, your faith, your relationships, your work, your past, your present, your future.

Second, if it sounds like fun, turn your journaling into a prayer, and *write a letter to God*. What do you want to say to God about that message you found in the in the text? What does this message make you want to say about your own life? Not everyone likes this kind of prayerful journaling, but if writing to God sounds fun, then go for it. Explain to God what the text seemed to say to you, and how it impacts your past, present, or future.

Third, if you want to step even further down the road of imagination, switch it around and *write a letter as if it is from God to you*. Imagine what God is saying to you personally based on the passage, your study, your sensory exercise, as well as your takeaway from the "Initial Writing Process" above. Is God sending you a message of comfort? A message of challenge? Of hope? Is God calling you to do something in particular? Write down whatever you imagine God saying. Afterward you'll have something to prayerfully consider—rich personal connections between the text and your life. Of course, you know this is your own imaginative writing exercise, not a direct word from God. But you may find that using your imagination in this way sparks something useful both for your life and for your sermon.

EXERCISE 4. LISTEN FOR THE MESSAGE IN YOUR CULTURE

The last exercise in this step is to move beyond your personal takeaway message to think about how that message is relevant to others—to people in your church and to our culture. Get out some more paper or your journal, and a pen. Get ready to brainstorm. Your goal is to come up with some familiar stories that connect to what you've learned and felt in this passage of Scripture. Your sermon is setting up a kind of conversation between the biblical text and the life we live today. Popular culture can give you tools to communicate about either side of that conversation.

On the biblical text: If you watch a lot of television, think about shows you've enjoyed — or films, or novels, or stories in the news, or even things in the shared experience of your congregation. With your text and your takeaway in mind, think about particular episodes, scenes, characters, and conflicts. Listen for things that illustrate some moment from the Bible story you are working on. Think about each character and situation, each conflict and resolution, each sin and each virtue. You might find echoes in our culture of any of these things and more in the text. What about the feelings people in the text might have experienced? Are there scenes from our culture that produce those same feelings in people?

On modern life: Scenes from popular culture can also be helpful in illustrating our own situations and struggles. Think of different life situations today where the text's message applies. Is there something in a film or novel that is similar? If the text evokes a particular emotion in you, is there something in a story you've read or seen that evokes a similar emotion? Any connection, even a slight one, is worth noting. Write down at least a phrase or two each time something comes to mind.

Why are you digging for this stuff? A good story is like a bridge between the world of our lives and the world of the Bible. That's why Jesus taught in parables. If the text sparks a reference to something in popular culture in your mind, chances are that same pop culture reference will help the people in your congregation connect their own lives to the text.

You don't need to think yet about

whether you will use these stories in your sermon. You are still just compiling relevant stories. You are drawing connections in your own mind and your notes between the text and real life. Then you'll be steeped in the sense that this text really connects, really matters for the life we live.

And don't worry if your list of stories is very short. Some people come up with this stuff easily, and for others it is harder going.

Then (drum roll, please) you are ready for step five. It's time to write your sermon.

STEP FIVE: BRINGING IT ALL TOGETHER

At last, you are finally ready to actually write your sermon. And I do want you to write the whole thing out. If you are new to preaching, chances are you are going to be nervous come Sunday morning. One thing that can really help calm your nerves is to know that every word you need to say is written down on paper, and you have that paper in your cold, clammy little hand.

Now here's the good news: All the work you've done in the earlier steps is going to make writing your sermon pretty easy. To make it even easier, I'm going to give you an organizational plan—a template of sorts. You do not even need to create the outline of your sermon.

This is not the only way to organize a sermon. It might not even be the best way. There are lots of ways to organize a sermon, truth be known. If you end up preaching a lot, you will probably pick up other approaches from books, from teachers, or just by listening to good preachers. Eventually, maybe even soon, you'll be thinking of your own ways to structure your sermons.

But with this sermon, your *first* sermon, we're aiming for *easy*. I can tell you this is a genuinely easy way to prepare a faithful and helpful sermon on your very first try—and if it is faithful to the text and helpful to the people, it will be a *successful* sermon. So, do it this way, just this one time. It will make your life easier.

THE GOAL: FOUR SPECIFIC PAGES

Here's what you are arming for:

- Four pages
- Each page dealing with one very specific topic
- All of it typed, double-spaced, in a 12-point font

The question "Why *four* pages?" is different from the question "Why *these* four pages?"

I'm not the first person ever to say your sermon should have four pages. In fact, there's a well-known book entitled *The Four Pages of a Sermon*. I've heard it is very good, but since I have not read it, I don't know how much my four-page template overlaps with that book's recommendations. If you end up preaching more regularly, I hope you'll check it out.

Four pages is a great length for your first sermon, in my opinion, because if you read your sermon at a measured pace, it will be twelve to sixteen minutes long. That is, reading at a pace slow enough for your congregation to listen, it will take you about three to four minutes to get through each double-spaced page of 12-point text. Twelve to sixteen minutes is long enough for the people to really get engaged with what you are saying. If you only have one or two pages, then just about the time the congregation gets fully tuned in to your channel, you'll be saying "Amen!" and sitting back down.

Having one full page for each subtopic is about right too. If you only say a sentence or two about something, half the congregation will miss it. Some people will be helping their squirrelly kids. Others will be blowing their noses. Still others will be distracted by all the squirmy kids and honking noses. That means you need to say a significant amount on any topic you want people to really hear. You shouldn't just make your point and move on. Fill up the page for each subtopic by making a point, and then looking at the same point from another angle, or illustrating it with a story. If you talk about something for a whole page, everybody can tune in for at least part of your point.

And why these four *particular* topics that I suggest for your pages? You'll see. These topics will lead the people through a natural process of engaging with the Scriptures and listening for what God is saying in them.

1. The congregation will start by taking in *the particular story* found in the text.

2. Then they will ponder some of the *puzzling, challenging, or curious* bits that make the text interesting.

3. Then they will consider ways this story and some of those interesting bits are *relevant to their lives* as Christians today.

4. Finally, they'll get a sense of how God is *calling* them, *blessing* them, or *challenging* them in this particular, puzzling, relevant text.

Sound reasonable? It should—all of your preparation has led to this. Let's get to it.

PAGE ONE: TELL THE STORY

Put a heading at the top, something like "Telling the Story." Only you will see this heading, but typing it there will keep you focused. On this page, tell the story in your own words, adding detail to make it engaging.

I'm serious when I say the first page of your sermon should retell the story of the text you probably just read to them. (If you didn't follow my advice to choose a Gospel text, don't worry. Think about other forms of "retelling," like paraphrasing an argument from Paul's letters or walking through a message from one of the prophets piece by piece.)

Why, you ask, should you spend your sermon time retelling a story that you just read out loud from the Bible two minutes before?

The simple answer is because they weren't paying attention the first time. Sure, some of the people were on the edge of their seats, gripped by every word. But the others? Not so much. Some zoned out for any one of a million reasons. Others don't ever feel that connected to the Bible; they've never read it, and they assume they would never understand it. And don't forget the squirrelly kids and the runny noses.

But even if everyone paid a reasonable amount of attention during the reading, you still need to retell it. They only heard it once. You studied it for hours. When you retell it in your own words, you can (and probably will) emphasize the little details, the repetitions, the odd turns of phrase that you found so important.

So, tell that story. Put it in your own words. Definitely don't just reread it. Bring in some of the details you imagined when you worked through it with your senses. That will help to make it vivid so that people become engaged. (What? You mean you ignored my advice to spend ten minutes imagining what every sense would experience if you had been there in the story? I'm shocked! Go back and do it now. It will make telling the story a whole lot easier.)

If the story is, say, the wedding at Cana, tell about how the bridegroom felt when he found out he hadn't bought enough wine. His face probably got hot and red, don't you think? Tell about Mary's tone of voice when she told Jesus the wine had run out. Talk about how Jesus may have felt and what his tone was when he told his mom that the lack of wine really wasn't his problem. Or tell about the sights and smells of a first-century Judean wedding banquet.

Flesh that story out so it sounds like real people doing real things for real reasons. It is okay to say what someone was thinking or feeling. This is storytelling, not critical scholarship. Help the congregation hear the story in a way that helps them notice what you found important in it.

If you find that you are short of a page, keep fleshing it out. It's fine to go over one page, but if you find yourself with a second full page for this section, you may need to trim. Hint: Delete things that draw people's attention away from the main thread.

PAGE TWO: EXPLORE THE PROBLEMS

Often, when you look very closely at a passage of Scripture, what seemed straightforward at first glance starts to look more and more confusing. I find that almost always one or several things in a Gospel story or parable begin to puzzle me. I suspect you found some things like this when you studied your passage. The second page of your sermon is the place to talk about some of those puzzling, challenging, curious bits. Put them out there on center stage for the congregation to see.

Put a heading at the top of your second page, something like "Exploring the Problems." Once again, only you will see this heading, but it will keep you on topic as you write, and when you preach, seeing it will remind you of what you are supposed to be talking about. Then write about the particular features or details that make this story interesting. If you write about several, end with one that leads into your main takeaway message. Then set up to transition to the third page by explaining how you made sense of it and how it gave you a sense of the text's important message.

To find these things, look back to the notes you put in the margins of the page you printed out after you broke down the structure of your text. (If you didn't follow my advice to break down the text into its logical and grammatical units, go back and do it now. Then spend some time doodling up its margins with your notes and observations. This is all about making it easier to write your sermon, so don't short change yourself.) Your study helped you find interesting things. Write about the best of them one by one.

It might seem counterintuitive to write about things you found confusing or problematic. You might think that the reason you studied so hard was to *solve* those problems, and that's true. Shouldn't you get up in the pulpit and talk about the solutions you found?

I'd say no, not yet. The congregation barely heard the story when you read it. When you retold it, they were just starting to get interested. They aren't immersed in the text like you are. They haven't begun to even notice the problems. If you solve the problems now, before they even know the problems are there, they won't really know how important your solution is.

They need an invitation to step inside the story. Help them notice the questions you found. Do that by bringing the congregation along as you ask questions of the text. In any subject, learning only happens when people ask questions. They'll learn only a bit if you start by answering the questions they haven't thought of yet. But if you help them see the problems, they will begin to ask questions of their own, and then they will be hooked. The challenges and puzzles of the text help them to be personally curious so they will be eager and open to the rest of your sermon. When they see some of the problems and questions, it's like when a novelist ends a chapter on a cliffhanger. The reader just has to turn the page and keep going.

Once again, if you come up short of a page for this exploration of problems, you need to flesh it out a bit. If you can't think of how to do that, try imagining your inner three-year-old whispering after every sentence "Why?" That little question will prompt you to find an answer.

- Why do you think that bit is

odd? Explain which details drew your attention.
- So why is that a problem? Explain what you expected, or what would have made more sense.
- But what does the text actually say? Why is that a problem? Explain the issues it raises.

Take the story of Jesus and the Syrophoenician woman—you know, the woman in Mark 7:24–30 whose daughter Jesus at first refuses to heal, saying he came for the children of Israel, not for the dogs. So why is that a problem? Jesus isn't kind to her. In fact, he seems pretty rude. Why is that a problem? Jesus is God in the flesh, and you expect God to be merciful and kind, or at least polite. Laying out the problem may require a little more storytelling or explaining your own expectations. Or maybe the problem is that it seems to contradict another passage of Scripture. Lay out the problem clearly so they notice it. Keep asking why and writing down the answers.

Just make sure by the end of the page you are focusing in on the very particular issue you found so important back in the study stage. If that issue is the solution to a particular problem, that makes it easy. Put that problem last, make it interesting, and slide into the solution, which presents your central message. You could say, "The problem that puzzled me most was [blank]. But in the end, I saw [blank]."

If your central message is not the solution to one of the problems you've been discussing, all is still well. Transition differently. You can say "As I wrestled with all these issues, one important message emerged clearly from the text." Then tell them what details in the text led you to find that message so weighty.

One warning on dealing with the text's puzzles and challenges in your sermon: Don't turn this page into a big complaint about how hard the process was. I've heard beginning preachers say in their sermons, "This was such a difficult text! I wrestled and struggled and didn't think I'd ever come up with a sermon!" It sounds like the preacher wants the congregation's pity. Talk about the text and its difficulties, not about yourself. Remember, the sermon is supposed to be about the text, not about you.

Actually, the congregation expects you to work hard. We expect the text to be challenging. Wrestling with the text is your job as the preacher—and it's a big job. Most people in the congregation are glad you were called to the task instead of them.

It is helpful to hear about the particular difficulties this text presents as we try to hear what God is saying. End on one difficulty that relates to the key message you want to focus on from this text. Then you can lead us toward your solution and that message. That's what pages three and four will do.

PAGE THREE: SHOW CONNECTIONS TO LIFE AND CULTURE

By the end of page two you were writing (and preaching) about the really interesting and useful message you found by studying this text. Now put a header at the top of page three that says something like "Connections to Real Life"—which, again, is just a reminder for you to keep you on track. Your job on page three is to tell a story or two that will illustrate aspects of the message you heard in the text.

You should give some careful thought about what goes on this page of your sermon. You are not looking for a joke, and you don't want just any story. You need a story that takes people a step or two deeper into the actual message of your sermon. The good thing is you have a whole list of possibilities for this section in your notes from step four—all those connections from TV shows, movies, books, the news, and from your own life.

Some preachers are convinced they need to include a joke in every sermon. I know of one preacher who thought that he needed to start every single sermon with a joke. This isn't stand-up comedy, it's preaching. Yes, humor is fun. When people laugh along with you, it feels like they are on your side. However, humor, on its own, is not actually *important*. What is important is relating the biblical text to our Christian lives. So if your joke (or story, or anything else) does not draw people into the *subject* of your sermon, it is a *distraction*.

That preacher who started every sermon with a joke made it hard for his congregation. As soon as the punch line was over, everyone had to shift gears internally. The joke had led them to think the sermon was on the topic of the joke. Once it was done, the preacher had to start all over, dragging them back in a different direction. If they laughed at the joke, the preacher had to work even harder to get the people to hear what he wanted to get across.

The stories you tell will be the most memorable things about your sermon. That's true, whether the stories are jokes, personal recollections, or bits from popular culture. This fact can be frustrating at times. You may long for them to grab hold of your hard-fought Bible insights, but they go home thinking about what you said about your old dog. Those Bible insights really are more *important* than the stories, but they are less *sticky*. It takes work for a congregation to focus and think with you about the Bible. But a story? Stories grab our attention and slide straight into our memory.

If you know the congregation will walk out remembering your story, what kind of a story do you want it to be? The answer to that should be easy: It needs to be a story that helps make your most important point.

This takes careful discernment. It also takes editing. I have some stories that I find intriguing and moving. Those stories creep into my first draft of sermon after sermon. I really want to share them. But then I ask myself, "Does this story help me make the point my sermon needs to make?" Time after time, the answer is no.

That's what the "delete" key is for.

In this, your first sermon, look for a story or two that does either of the following two things:

1. A good story might give an *example of the human problem* your text addresses.

2. A good story might give an example of the *solution to the problem* your text provides.

If your story does one of these things, then get ready to write it into your sermon.

If your story is from a book or movie or TV show, you'll need to provide a bit of context. Give just enough big picture or background so the people who didn't read or see it can still get the point.

On the other hand, if it's a story from real life, you'll need to take a bit of care. If that real-life story features someone from the congregation or from your family, ask permission before you tell it in public. You may think it is totally innocent or even cute. Your spouse, your child, or a church member may think differently. Some people would be deeply embarrassed simply to be named in such a public way, whatever the story, and you don't want to hurt the people you love. Also, think carefully before preaching a story that features you in the role of hero. It can be totally cringe-worthy when it sounds like the point of the story is to make the preacher look good.

As in the previous sections, if you are coming up short of a page here, you should think about fleshing out your story. Given the number of ways people can be distracted (remember the squirrelly kids and sneezy noses?), it isn't going to hurt to add words that make your point obvious. Telling the story, then telling them why you told the story, and pointing out exactly how it illustrates your very important point, can really help. Make sure your hearers have a chance to tune in and hear why you are telling the story. Does it give a helpful example of the human temptation or sin or struggle your text addresses? Then say so: "This problem that Jesus is talking about reminds me of a movie I saw."

You might also want to add another story. It might be wise to have a story of some kind for each of the two purposes I suggested: one to highlight the life problem the text points to, and one to highlight the potential solution or growth process that the text points to.

As to length, make sure each story is more like a paragraph than just a sentence or two. You need to give the people enough time to tune in before you move on. And spending a good solid page on stories that help listeners make personal connections with your text is a serious investment in the success of your sermon.

Here's a summary of my simple guidelines for stories:

- About a page of stories and connections.
- Nothing off topic.
- Nothing that makes you the hero.

- Something to see the faith problem suggested by the text.
- Something to help show the solution suggested by the text.

Then you are ready to bring it all home with page four.

PAGE FOUR: EMPHASIZE GOD'S CALL TO US

On the last page of your sermon, your job is to re-emphasize the message you found in the text, presenting it as God's call to us today. You can now easily do that by connecting it clearly to the situations we in the congregation actually feel. You know, stuff from your stories. Put a heading up at the top for yourself—something like "God's Call to Us Today."

The temptation is to just wrap up in a sentence or two: "Okay then! Let's all go love our neighbors!" *You need to do something more here.* You need to help the congregation process all the good stuff you've been talking about, reminding them of the crucial moment or teaching from the Bible passage. You need to remind them of how this issue is something they face in the real world, and that in this text the Lord gives us something wise and helpful about living faithfully in that situation.

The tone and content of this page will vary a lot depending on the kind of message you discerned in the text. Is the passage offering you a bit of healing or blessing? You'll want to joyfully offer that gift and help them joyfully receive it. Is the passage offering a challenge, or maybe a judgment on some well-established habit? Presenting that challenge requires something else, including gentleness and humility.

There are countless possibilities for the message God might be offering in a particular passage, to a particular congregation, through a particular preacher. My recommendation is that you return to the advice of the wise old preacher in the joke I told in step two. You've already prepared for the second part of that advice: to preach about 15 minutes. Now, on the last page, make sure you do what he advised first: to preach about Jesus.

Ask yourself some questions like,

- "What do I *learn about* Jesus here?"
- "What does Jesus show me in this story *about a common situation* in the life of faith?"
- "What do Jesus' words or actions *show me about how to live more faithfully* in that situation?"

- "What is Jesus *calling us to, or offering us*, in this passage?"
- "What do I want to *do to respond in faith* and faithfulness to Jesus here?"

Those questions may seem pretty familiar from previous steps in your preparation, or from earlier pages you've written for your sermon. That's just fine. It's actually a good thing. What you need to do is recap, and to do so specifically in relation to Jesus. Remind people of the journey they've been on as they listened to God through listening to this text. If you write a sentence or a short paragraph in answer to all or some of those questions, especially if you end with the last two, you may find you have written pretty much exactly what you need to bring the sermon to a good and useful conclusion.

The congregation will hear you summarize what Jesus is saying today in our context through the ancient words of this passage. They will hear how you personally want to respond to that message. Then they will be able to make the very short leap to how they want to respond to Jesus themselves.

Then put down your pen, or hit save and close your computer, and pray. Thank God for helping you write a sermon. Ask God to continue to help you on Sunday and to help the people be blessed by it.

Then rejoice, because you're done! Now all you have to do is actually preach it.

Good news: I have some tips for that too. That's what the last chapter is about.

STEP SIX: ACTUALLY PREACHING IT

Okay, you are probably thinking there should not be a sixth step in what I promised would be a five-step process.

Plus, if I promised that the steps would be "manageable," then it shouldn't include public speaking. Lots of people list public speaking among their worst fears, so how can preaching your sermon be "manageable?" Well, I could say that all the manageable steps were about preparation, and you have done them. But you knew public speaking was part of the deal when you agreed to preach on Sunday. Right?

The question is, how can we make the actual preaching of the sermon manageable —or at least as manageable as possible? Well, rejoice and be glad: I have eight pro tips for you, all designed to build your confidence and reduce your anxiety.

1. PRINT IT LEGIBLY

The first thing to do is to print your sermon out. You'll want to have the whole thing up there with you on Sunday morning.

You may have a pastor who preaches with no notes at all. Don't try that on your first sermon. Standing in front of the congregation without the safety net of a manuscript puts a huge amount of pressure on. Save that for later. Much later.

Writing the whole thing out was partly a way to help you think clearly about what you want to say. Best to do that when there is less pressure and more time to think. I wanted to help you avoid trying to preach off the cuff, making up words while everyone is staring at you.

Now that you have written those words, I want you to print them out because it helps to have them with you in the pulpit. It's a huge confidence builder. When you stand up there and look out at all those faces, you might just forget everything you wanted to say. It has happened. But if you have your manuscript, all you have to do when you go blank is look down and see what the next sentence is.

But here's the real insider's advice: Blow that text up. You typed it into a file using a standard 12-point font to get the length right. Before you print it, change the font to something bigger. Use a larger font, something in the range of 16- to 20-point, so you can easily read it without squinting or holding it up close. If you wear bifocals, you don't want to be bobbing your head to look through that special spot where you can see fine print.

2. USE THE PULPIT

When you preach, stand behind the pulpit. You may have a pastor who wanders all over the room while preaching. Don't do that on your first sermon either.

Why? Well, for one thing, you are planning to bring your manuscript with you. Standing in the middle of the room and leafing through a handful of papers while trying to preach could serve as the dictionary definition of "awkward." Worse still, you might drop them. And remember, your pastor is familiar with maneuvering around up there while everybody watches. You don't want to trip and tumble down the stairs.

The pulpit is a very useful piece of furniture for a preacher. It provides you with a perfect place to set your papers down right where you can see them. Plus, a pulpit can give a nervous preacher a bit of psychological protection. Nobody can see your knees shaking behind the pulpit.

And believe it or not, everyone will hear you better if you are standing the pulpit. Pulpits weren't invented to make the preacher look authoritative. Back before microphones and amplification, pulpits helped congregations hear the sermon. They put you a step or two up, right in everyone's line of sight. Your voice travels to peoples' ears more easily without heads, hats, and hairdos blocking the journey of the sound waves.

3. PRACTICE

You can build your confidence further by reading your sermon aloud. That's true whether you have someone listening to you or not. Ideally you should do this a few times. Get used to the sound of those words and sentences rolling off your tongue.

Have a pencil with you when you practice so you can mark any bits that sound odd. Your ear may notice typos or grammar problems that your eye missed. You will probably find things that look fine in print but sound convoluted out loud, or words that are harder to pronounce than you think they will be.

English may be just one language, but most people write it differently from the way they speak it. Learning to write for the ear instead of the eye is something that usually has to grow over time. When you write your first sermon, your sentences may be way too long. Or you may place the verb or the subject of sentences in awkward places. Your ear will catch this stuff. After you've read it and marked it up, go back to your computer and fix the things you didn't like. Then print it out again.

Next, try reading your sermon with a timer. If you find yourself coming to the end in only ten minutes or so, try it again reading much more slowly. Lots of us normally talk too fast for a congregation, and many people speed up when they are nervous. That makes it really important to practice reading slowly. You'll probably find you need to read at a pace that feels way too slow. That's okay. The point is, you need to give the people a chance to hear and understand.

You are so familiar with what you wrote that you may find yourself just rattling through in no time. Keep in mind that the congregation will be hearing these words for the first and only time. Listening to someone read a sermon from the pulpit is a very different experience from reading those pages with your own eyes. When reading for yourself, you set your own pace. If it is a familiar subject, your eye can dance along pretty quickly. Likewise, if you miss something, your eye can stop and re-read a word or a sentence.

When listening to a sermon with your ears, you can't go back and re-listen except in your memory. Imagine that you think you missed a bit of the sermon. You stop to think about the sentence that confused you. While thinking about that last sentence, your brain is occupied; your ears basically turn off. When you tune your ears back in, you find you missed two more entire sentences.

Result? More confusion.

Solution? When preaching, read slowly and clearly. Give them all a chance to hear your stories, your questions, your insights.

4. TRY OUT THAT PULPIT IN ADVANCE

If at all possible, go into the church before the service and stand in the pulpit. Practice the whole thing there if you can. Even if you can't do a practice run in the pulpit, get familiar with the feeling of standing there, looking out where the congregation will be. See what your manuscript looks like sitting there in front of you.

All this pre-service stuff is an attempt to eliminate surprises. The more you do before the service to become familiar with the sermon itself and the place you will preach it, the fewer issues you have to be nervous about.

5. SPEAK TO THE LAST ROW

There is one more variable you can work on in advance: your voice. You need to get used to hearing yourself talk in that big worship space, and you need to learn to talk so that you can be heard.

While you are there checking out the pulpit sometime before the service, ask somebody to sit in the very last row. Then do a personal sound check. Speak to that person from the pulpit. Ask if they can hear you clearly. So long as the person in that last row can hear you, everyone in between can hear too. You don't need to even use your sermon for this. You could just have a conversation. Or you could read the Bible passage. You just have to hear your own voice and be confident that you will be heard.

If that friend in the back row can't hear you clearly, though, you need to speak louder. Teaching you to project your voice is beyond what I can do in this little book. However, the best way to speak more loudly has two parts: First, use your stomach muscles to push your breath out while you speak. If your breath flows from your chest, your voice will be very soft, so pull that stomach in while you talk. Second, at the same, time keep your throat relaxed so your voice sounds open and resonant, as opposed to sounding squeezed or pinched. But if doing all of that seems daunting, just make your voice louder any old way you can.

6. GIVE YOURSELF PERMISSION TO BE NERVOUS

On Sunday morning it is very likely that you will be nervous. I know people who have preached for decades and still find themselves facing an upset stomach every Sunday before service.

The trick is to give yourself permission to be nervous. If you don't, you might just make it worse by condemning yourself for it. It's okay to be nervous. You are doing something important. It's your first time. Plus, you are doing it in public. Being nervous is human. Just be kind to yourself about it, and keep moving forward. Know that God is with you. And know that the people in the congregation are your friends. They are all rooting for you.

7. FIND A FRIENDLY NODDER

I have one really excellent tip to calm your nerves and ensure that everything goes well: Find someone in the congregation who smiles and nods.

This is not the typical advice for public speakers. You've probably heard someone say that of you are nervous about public speaking, you should picture the audience in their underwear. No. Please, no. That's just gross. And inappropriate. Personally, seeing that vision from the pulpit would make me even more uncomfortable.

You'll do better to scan the crowd for someone who looks really kind and really interested. If I can find someone who is smiling warmly as he or she listens, I know that at least one person really wants to hear what I have to say. That puts me totally at ease.

One friendly smiler counteracts the effect of the grumpy guy sitting there in the third row with his arms crossed. Of course, in my mind I know that his grumpiness is probably not about me. Still, when I'm preaching and I see him scowl, I assume that he absolutely disagrees with my every point. Likewise, of course, the smiler may not be smiling about my insightful sermon at all. Even so, the smile *feels* supportive.

The truly ideal person is not just a smiler, but a smiling *nodder*. In my preaching, and even more in my teaching, I often talk without sticking to my manuscript or notes. When I find someone who nods in understanding, often a kindly looking woman, she clues me in that I've made my point. That way I can move on. Otherwise I'll keep explaining the same point for five more minutes.

Even if you stick to your sermon manuscript to the letter, the smiling nodder will help you, calm you, put you at ease. You can think "Hooray! At least one person gets it! Somebody likes my sermon!"

That's your real pro tip: Find the friendliest face in the room, and speak the entire sermon just to that person. Everyone else will hear it too, but put your attention on the person who is helping you feel at ease.

8. THEN STOP

When you get to the end, you can just sit down, or say "Amen!" or lead them in a little prayer for help in living in response to God's message in the passage. Whatever your style, you're done, so sit back down. While the service rolls toward its end, talk with God inside your heart. Thank God for the opportunity to participate in the amazing process of preaching. Pray that God's message will be heard through your words, and even despite your words.

(I say "despite your words" because sometimes God seems to get his own message across regardless of what you say from the pulpit. Most preachers have had the strange experience of someone coming up after the service to say thanks for some very particular message that you know for a fact never came out of your mouth.)

Once you are at that point, remember my last word to you: *congratulations!* You did it. You preached a sermon that was faithful to the biblical message and helpful to your congregation. That's something to be proud of.

However, if you've read this book to the end before doing the steps, I suggest you do one of two things.

1. You could go back and read through the book again, doing each step before turning to the next chapter.

2. Or, if you want a bit more support in the process, turn the page for some offers that can get you there.

But once you have actually preached your sermon, I hope you'll tell me how it went. Just drop me a line at Gary@GaryNealHansen.com.

AFTERWORD

I'm so glad you decided to read my little book on preparing and preaching your first sermon. I know, though, that some people learn better by listening and seeing or through a helpful conversation instead of just reading. If that is you, I have three options to offer you on my video course, "Your First Sermon: Getting from Here to Sunday in Five Manageable Steps." You'll find a link to the course on my website, or to go there directly use https://bit.ly/PreachingClass.

Once you get there, choose the level you want to sign up for, and enter the specified coupon code for that level when you check out. (Note that the letters are all capitals, and the numbers are ordinary numerals.)

Option 1: $10 off the basic level of the course (five video lessons, with manageable step-by-step instructions to get your sermon done by Sunday). **Coupon code:** LP-BGISEMD7

Option 2: $15 off the medium level (five video lessons as above, *plus feedback on your sermon manuscript* before you have to preach it). **Coupon code:** BGF88C6MI4

Option 3: $20 off the super-duper level (full video course and sermon manuscript feedback as above, *plus a half-hour coaching call* to help your preparation). **Coupon code:** 7NU5EMMYT5

If one of those sounds helpful, go for it! I really want you to succeed.

SUGGESTIONS FOR FURTHER READING

If you decide to keep at this preaching thing, here are a few books to help you take you to the next level.

John R. W. Stott. *Between Two Worlds: The Challenge of Preaching Today*. Downers Grove, IL: InterVarsity Press, 1982. Reprint edition, 2017.

Thomas G. Long, *The Witness of Preaching*, third edition. Louisville: Westminster John Knox Press, 2016.

Paul Scott Wilson. *The Four Pages of the Sermon*, revised and updated. Nashville: Abingdon Press, 2018.

Barbara Brown Taylor. *The Preaching Life*. Plymouth, UK: Cowley Publications, 1993.

ACKNOWLEDGMENTS

I offer my very sincere thanks to my supporters on Patreon: John Armstrong, April Saber Asad, Jack Craft, Viola Duff, Edwin Lacy, Nick Marlatt, Claudia McFie, Stephen Nichols, Reneé Notkin, and Gary Panetta. Your generosity made this book happen.

Thanks to Teddi Black (teddiblack.com) for designing the cover, and to Rebecca Cooper for her editorial work.

Thanks to Rebecca Senkowicz, who taught my kids to swim while I sat by the Magee Pool and wrote the first draft of this book in the summer of 2019.

And special thanks to my wife, Dawna Duff, for reading the manuscript and providing helpful feedback.

OTHER BOOKS BY GARY NEAL HANSEN

Kneeling with Giants: Learning to Pray with History's Best Teachers

Love your Bible: Finding Your Way to the Presence of God with a 12th Century Monk

Christmas Play

Illuminate-Your-Own Gospel of Mark

Illuminate-Your-Own Gospel of Matthew

In the "Being Reformed" adult education curriculum series:

Church History: Those Who Shaped the Church Participants Book

The Heidelberg Catechism Participants Book

Subscribe to Gary's weekly newsletter at http://bit.ly/GaryNealHansenNewsletter to get all his new articles and announcements.

Made in the USA
Monee, IL
24 April 2021